Theatre Poems and Songs

This volume is Edward Bond's own selection (in collaboration with the editors) of over one hundred of his poems and songs. They are all linked with his work as a playwright and cover the years 1968 to 1977. They fall into three groups. The first consists of poems and songs from plays, an opera and a ballet. The second group is of pieces which were part of the creative process of evolving a finished work – an unusual form of notes on work in progress which give a unique commentary on the sources and impulses behind the plays and on why they developed as they have. Many of these pieces are richly revealing of the author's state of mind when writing and of his attitudes to the characters and situations he was creating. Lastly there is a group of poems written after the completion of a play and which are the author's reflections and commentaries on the finished work. Many of these last pieces were originally written for theatre programmes.

All the poems and songs offer in varying ways views of the plays and of the function of the theatre. Together they represent an important series of insights into one of the most powerful and accomplished writers of our time.

The photograph of Edward Bond on the front cover is from a photo by Tony McGrath.

Edward Bond

Theatre Poems and Songs

edited by Malcolm Hay
and Philip Roberts

EYRE METHUEN
London

To Betty and Robert

822.91
B711t

First published 1978 by Eyre Methuen Ltd
11 New Fetter Lane London EC4P 4EE
Copyright © 1978 by Edward Bond
Printed in Great Britain by
Cox & Wyman Ltd,
London, Fakenham and Reading

ISBN 0 413 45420 7 (Hardback)
ISBN 0 413 45430 4 (Paperback)

209660

CONTENTS

We Come to the River

Author's Note

The poems, songs and choruses in this book are arranged under the titles of plays and an opera and a ballet I have written or (in the case of *Spring Awakening*) translated.

They fall into three groups. Firstly, those that are part of a play or music work. These are printed in bold type and come from my plays *Narrow Road to the Deep North*, *Passion*, *Stone* and *Grandma Faust*, from the opera *We Come to the River* (set to music by Hans Werner Henze) and from an unscored ballet. The second group is of poems written to be printed in theatre programmes when the related play or music work is performed. They were written after the play or music work had been finished and are a commentary on it or a guide to it. Thirdly there is a group of pieces written in notebooks or on work sheets (and sometimes on paperbags, cardboard boxes and other things that were to hand) when I was planning or writing a play or music work. These 'notebook' poems were part of the creative effort of writing the finished work but they are not part of the finished work and were not intended to be. These are here published for the first time and are printed in italics.

All the pieces were written over the last ten years. I have revised some of them for this book. They are printed in roughly the order in which they were first written. The chief exception to this is the poems from *Narrow Road to the Deep North*. These were written before the *Lear* poems but are here printed after them. Some have already been published in the working class magazine *Fireweed* and others in a broadsheet by *Inter-Action*.

I thank Malcolm Hay and Philip Roberts for their help in selecting and editing the pieces for the book and Nick Hern for his care and patience in preparing it for publication.

Edward Bond

Lear

Lear

Lear

Lear was born in ancient shadow
When men stumbled in darkness
And bound their wounds with myths

In scene one Lear suffers The Great Vice
Fear
And so commits The Three Great Crimes
Cruelty arrogance and rhetoric

He's shot on the wall
At death he began to make a new life
Others still live the old life

The Bastille was stormed from without
We storm the prison from within
No man stands outside to throw it down
Those who sit inside and don't know it's a prison
Are gaolers

Our world is not absurd – our society is
Art is rational and subverts the past
When the weak choose to fight they are already strong
A man's pessimism is measured by what he will lose
His hope by what he will gain
When the world is changed

This play is guerilla in the theatre
But because this is theatre
You are handed this poem

To the Audience

You sit and watch the stage
Your back is turned –
To what?

The firing squad
Shoots in the back of the neck
Whole nations have been caught
Looking the wrong way

I want to remind you
Of what you forgot to see
On the way here
To listen to what
You were too busy to hear
To ask you to believe
What you were too ashamed to admit

If what you see on the stage displeases
You run away
Lucky audience!
Is there no innocence in chains
In the world you run to?
No child starving
Because your world's too weak
And all the rich too poor
To feed it?

On the stage actors talk of life and imitate death
You must solve their problems in your life
I remind you
They show future deaths

On Leaving the Theatre

Do not leave the theatre satisfied
Do not be reconciled

Have you been entertained?
Laughter that's not also an idea
Is cruel

Have you been touched?
Sympathy that's not also action
Corrodes

To make the play the writer used god's scissors
Whose was the pattern?
The actors rehearsed with care
Have they moulded you to their shape?
Has the lighting man blinded you?
The designer dressed your ego?

You cannot live on our wax fruit
Leave the theatre hungry
For change

Titles

Not a passport to tell the audience
The play will make no disturbance in the mind
And so may be given entry

Not a label of contents
But a direction for the journey
'Fragile' or 'This Way Up'

The opening date in a war or action
Followed by a dash and a question mark

A twitch in the corpse's face
That delays the Inspector's report

Not the name on the spectator's tombstone
(In the past we went to the theatre to be buried
Culture sounded like a sermon
So we thought we ought to be buried there)
But the miles on a signpost

> And he who hesitates is lost
> Even though he takes the right road

Lear's Song

Daughters should be stones worn smooth by fathers' tears
I have wept away mountains with my tears
But my daughters are jagged and cut feet
My daughters hide in cracks in stones
They suck the tears from my eyes
I am blinded by my daughters' sucking
They spit my tears at the people
I am old and incontinent with weeping
The king should be housetrained
He shall not wet his loins or his face
Both dirts shall be trained away
But I weep
My daughters are witches
They turn my tears to blood
I am incontinent with blood
They have locked me away
My blood seeps out under the door
They will kill me
I am a ghost haunting a mirror
I am incontinent with death
They have drained my death into a glass
My daughters have put it before me on this table
I am the space between iron bars
My daughters have carried me
In their belly
And on their shoulders to my grave

Lear's Father

My father
Is a dust path
That leads to a desolate place
On the side of a mountain

Below, a tarn
A bird falls
Rakes the water with claws
And rises with flakes of light
The boulders are bodies covered from disaster

His groans and the nightjar mix
I watch:
He is mad
The waterfall rustles
He searches the empty papers
Always for nothing, nothing
And drops them
Searching and weeping

But this is the place where he lived
Made thin corn grow from dust
This is the stone where he killed
He called it the killing stone
This is the path he made with his feet
Once he walked up the hill but turned back
This is the house he made – now ruins
This is the place he cleared for arrows

He shouted and stoned birds in the morning
Wore rags of wool and hair
Was drunk with water
He walked as if following a coffin looking at dust
He danced like an enemy
And his children played with his skeleton
Whistling his bones while he worked
Too old to be born

This is the place where he fell
Blood on his own field
If they had buried him then!
But they hoisted him through the streets
They pulped his hair for paper
They covered their feet with his skin
His bones are rods and his teeth are dice
They eat what they can and build with the rest

Lear's Prison

Mammoth sabre tooth tiger
Moth and dragon
Stood guard over young men before
Hunted and mated
In snow and desert
Lifted head at movement
Pricked ears at sound
Saw life death play terror
Stood up at dawn
Stood still by water
Hid in storm
Howled before men
Died before men
Chained to earth but bird
Ended dead on earth but ran
Timeless
Experience of itself
A staff cut before men
A ring worn before women

Then man took guard over his watch
A void ghost
A space and the world prowled round in him
The prison

Lear at Forty

His face white
Tall brow
Dark eyes

Staring at the distance –
The spot between the hills
Where the enemy came

His clothes clink
When he puts them on

The woman in dark
Puzzled him
Most felt
When nothing seen

His children on wooden horses
That sway like living trees

At thirty three
He met the fool
He saw him outside
Vomiting on
The wall of the judgement hall
'I must hang murderers
To save the innocent
I am not excessive'
'More than one
Today then . . .?'

Dead soldiers in a field
Face up and down to right and left
The night came on

Panic in the eyes of the singer
When the trumpet joined in

One time he remembered
The sound of his boots long ago
Walking on leaves

Out in a boat
He told the rowers to stop
And listen to silence

He no longer heard
The fool
He knew
All the jokes

On parade
Suddenly had to stand tiptoe
To see over his daughters

But he saw
In the corner of his eye
The fool had taken
A new lease of life
Brisker when older
(Looks made-up)

How noisy the dogs at the hunt!
Did they always snap at each other's
Hindquarters while we drank
The stirrup cup
And was the fox always already dead
When it jumped on the hill?

In the coffin she looked
Twice-burnt ash
His daughters entertained
And tended her grave
On one day

And then he forgot
The grammatical form
Of questions
Instead
Studied how
To stand stones on end

The machine must be regulated
The bishops blessed
The magicians bribed
The army kept
Under its shield

In an empty cup
After the dark wine tempest . . .
And outside nothing

I will go to the judgement hall
Shut the door on the fool
I took a handkerchief from my pocket
And the sky came out
Is that gap under the door
The fool's eye?

Song of the Grave Digger's Boy

I am the wisest owl
I am the lion that sleeps with lambs
Shadow is not chained to my feet
It blossoms from me
It is my cupped body for infants
I am the faun with the pride of lions
I am the snake that makes music in grass
Trees root in my hands
I am the bird that sharpens its beak on ears of ripe corn
I walk before antelope
The spider spins its web in my eye
Radiance!
The snake vanishes into my ear at thunder
Lice breed and burn away under my nails
My tongue is green
My vessels are roots

When the man points his bloody gun at me
I end his faint with his tears
A woman like heaps of rags rises in fright when I come from the
    trees
Her hands!
This wet is the blood of snow
For stones weep when we walk on them

I will not close my eyes to this echo of blood
It is shed and each sound in the clock is the drop of it
A clock is a grave with a gun pointed at it
That is the city walls and the keep
I am a live target
When blood drips from the ends of guns
I do not run to kill it

The Snake

Bright snake
Disembowelling earth with each movement
Wounding light with your eyes
Miser counting gold on fingers inside your body
You cannot be killed
The blood from your murder
Would seep on my pillow at night
Appear on the table before my guests
You still feed on birds in sunny afternoons
Fetching them through the bars of their cage
For you death is a moment's delay
An inconvenience
You live by spilling blood as men exhale who breathe

Why then now we have met on this path
And there's no more rustling in dark leaves
Shall I not strike
Taking on blood
As I am already cursed with your death?

The Autopsist and the Fish

The autopsist enters the number of corpses
Each night
In his book

In the morning the book of corpses
Is read in the square
To the waiting workers

Each worker will supply
Ten fingers two arms
Two feet two legs
So that the autopsist
May check his watch

Some bodies
Vanish under the bridge
Into the swirling of water
And the silver fish
Tear bits from their sides
Where the weeds move slowly
Like damp fires in the water

Men on the bridge
Watch this wreckage for fish

The Human Form

How wonderful is the human form
How robust the man
Abundant the woman
How shrewd the human eye
How fecund the brain
How like a book the tongue
What a gimlet is the eye
The mind strong and subtle as water
To it corners are twists in the wind
And we are named not numbered
The prints on our fingers are not police codes

Why therefore are our hands in chains
And our smiles so often without knowledge?

Narrow Road to the Deep North

Narrow Road to the Deep North

The Old Horse

The old horse stops on the bridge
The carter unhitches and leads her from the shafts
Leg broken
Passers-by help to push her in the river
Wild struggle but she drowns quickly
Floats at rest
Head down, mane in eyes
The carter goes off between the shafts

The Soldier

The soldier leant his spear on the wall
It fell
Clatter
They took him in for idleness

On Being Arrested

Two soldiers came
The head of the city wants me
They waited
While I wrote this poem

Poems Kiro Reads

1.
A feather falls from the sky
There are no birds here
The nests are broken and
The migration's over

2.
The soil was dry
The flower bent its petal mouth
To drink
The soil was still dry

3.
I drain the cup
At the bottom
Flags!

Black Mass

Black Mass

Black Mass

Bird

Fly on bird!
Over the winter city in ruins of snow
The beggar with broken wrists
The tannoy that learns speech

Fly on!
Past men with heads for faces
In cars like snakes fleeing water
One book for rules and another for writing in

Fly on!
Past time with a hatchet
The member washing blood from under his nails
The youth who says: I go along for the ride
And climbs on the gallows cart

Their glittering corn is deadlier than famine
Their water is dust and chokes cities
Sentimentality covers cynicism in their beds

Fly on blackbird!
With claw smashed through beak
Skull cracked
Wings like burned flags
Charred cracked firework
Fly on! Fly on!

Your hands give birth to children
And hold men waiting death
These are small things
If the sky is not lived in the earth dies

I Cannot Mourn

I cannot mourn men killed at Sharpeville
How can I mourn when I have to ask who they are?
Faces I haven't seen, unrecognizeable in dust anyway
Voices I haven't heard, the screams could be anyone's
Hands fighting death, making gestures you see in pictures
How can I mourn when I can't believe it happened?
How can I believe men shot parents running to hold their
      children?
How can I believe men shot children?
What men shoot children in the back?

But I understand when I see it like this:
Sharpeville isn't a village
It isn't even a nation
It's an effect that follows a cause
Be afraid like that
Covet like that
Hate like that
Believe in the armed state
As the font of all wisdom
And the effect follows
Sharpeville is very simple
The sentry must challenge the dark and shoot the mountain
The righteous must have their victim

Then the bodies are stacked at my door
I step over them in the street when I go home
I wake and they're piled at my window

The Rest

The body falls
An X marking itself
Buries under its own weight
In its own shadow
Under the horizon in its narrowed eyes
And rests

We wander from stretcher to table to fire
Faded like flowers and wire and cards
Using our death rattles as slogans
Why do we say let it rest?

The old bitch in her ivory tower
Makes trials out of funerals
Calls dead to the stand
To swear she is virgin in body and mind
She doesn't rest!

Run quickly and breathe their last breath!
Sing in their argument!
Dance in their stillness!
They have taken away the rest
And left us the lotus gun

Passion

Passion

A Dead Soldier's Thoughts

My tanks set fire to corn
My bullets stripped trees
I made where I was a grave
And walked and laughed in it
Once in a little quiet
I watched a singing bird build a nest
In the cardboard boxes we use to put bodies in

My flares blind stars
My guns shatter thunder
I ravaged more than plagues and famine
My bayonet was sharp
Whetted on blood and cries of unpitied men
I crippled to make men happy
Built prisons to set them free
The simpleton drooling in a bath-chair inherited
        under my will
I am the father of millions of orphans

I am dead
The bird sang when blood ran out of my arms
It sings still
My grave is a cage and it has the sky
If I could rise now on wings
I would sing
I would sing

Madmen peace!
You who bend iron but are afraid of grass
Peace!

The dust on my wings shines in the sun
I have learned to sing in winter and dance in my
    shroud
I have learned that a pig is a form of a lamb
Madmen, you are the fallen!

The Sea

The Sea

Spring

A white spider hangs in the blossom
Its red eyes are pips of death
It dances and leaps in the wind
A madman casting his silver entrails
Possessed by spring
The pink dome of its mouth
A cathedral roof
Under it aztecs sucking blood

The apple is a machine
The wood has coffins and tables in it
Spring! Spring!
The sun gives the trees
Bright armour

Seasons

How gentle the terrible seasons come and go
Each one measuring out merely one length
Like a man prostrate before a king or pope
Summer never attacking the house of winter
Autumn never digging up the bones of spring
The vast clouds piling upon their littler selves
To fall

What are the terrible seasons that pass so gently?
The iron vice of anger
That holds its threat for generations
The frown that becomes its own repose
The path worn in the small garden of the prison
Round and round
Close to the wall
To open out space
The tyrant bequeathing death in his will
Sending his living hearsemen
Through houses and streets and open places
Trailing ropes –
     These are not seasons

The black storm
Ice shattering its skull at night
Flood carrying roots at its head –
     These are the mild seasons

The mild seasons come and go
And in the change we live
As a travelling ship
Tosses from side to side
On unending waves

Only water can balance air
Only air rest on water
Only such lightness carry
The weight of the world

A Mad Man

The mad man stood beside the road
His face was a white bag with holes
Punched in for eyes

His hands were broken tools
The rivets had dropped out
There was a sign-post behind him

He had once built ships or cars
Or counted money in a book
He had once tried to feel his wife
But a net makes everything feel the same
Hang and move in the same way
Smell of sea shocked when it's dragged up into air

She moved inside the green net
Like despair
The water dripping
Whether she moved or not
Onto the wet stones

Everything caught in a net
Looks and tastes and moves like wet bread
And smells of the sea's old age

Her

I do not have to be too nice to her
I treat her as I treat myself
Asking all my desires
And answering with my passions
So that from time to time
I come to peace
In her

The water goes down to the deeper sea
Calling in the dark waters
The moon shines on flecks of panic
The huge current under the ocean
Drowns despair and death
And is as silent as the way between
The stars

She is my life
I offer her my breath

Love Song

Away over the ocean
Where the sea-seeds grow
I look

You are so near
But to see you the eye goes
To the horizon

Deeper

To reach you the gesture is huge
Shaped by seasons

The simple music
Is stiller, less listless
Than silence
Where you are

Spring Awakening

Spring Awakening

The QC

It is the democratic right
Of the judge
To be forgiven
By the prisoner

For without mercy
How could the judge
Ride home in safety?

Juvenile Delinquents

The Prince of Wales
Is driven
To Mansion House
On taxpayers' money
To waffle clichés
Banal by any standards
On the duty
Of leadership

Then goes off
To shoot grouse
On taxpayers' money

Skinheads break street lamps
Savages!

Teachers

To teach children
A culture that's also
A way of life
To stop hooligans
Destroying
When that's
The only act
Of creation they can prove
Works
You must have
In every school
This ratio:
    One teacher to six pupils

But where
Can we get
So many teachers?

At present
They're running
Borstals and prisons
And working
In vast factories

Making narcoticising gadgetry
To control
The Eat-All society
Because you don't have
This ratio:
    One teacher to six pupils

rithmetic Lesson

one bomb kills
wo million men
Iow many bombs does it take
o kill . . .

hool Visit to Factory

urning that nut
ighter
he car rolls slowly forward
he man stands still

e've made it easy
or our workers

Iorning Prayers

God
et Sir's team win
men

he Hitler Salute

ne hand raised now
ater two
r clutching a hole
the chest

Officer Cadet Training Corps

Why do men
Plant so carefully
The tree on which
They will hang?

A Dead Soldier at Verdun

I have become
The earth I fought for
Who will walk over it
Or own the fruit
That grows here?

A Lesson

German Brutes
Before the Great War
Covering empty ideas
With thick words
Sexual hypocrisy
For the Fatherland
Preparing children
With canes
For bayonets
And Gatling guns

So, an academic culture
Too illiterate
To decipher
Its own epitaph

And we?

Teach children
A culture they mustn't touch
Say: create
But later only: work
Say: bodies
Without ideas
Die
And offer: colour
On TV

But they are free to choose?
So push a man
From the ship
And say: swim

The teacher's book
May be the All Truth
But the act of teaching it
Is a lie
When the social machine
Is built from battery people
Who consume and make
But can't stop to reflect
What profit is drawn
From their treadmill:
    The privilege
    Of money or power or pride

Men are trapped by their needs
And obey when
Others own
Their means of living
And therefore their
Wives and mothers and children

But the child
To grow
Needs self respect
Integrity
Having no other obligations:
   It's as simple as that

So the child creates
His own culture
Primitive for the jungle
Violent for the fight
Hopeless for his chances

In the prison hulks
Of the great city schools
He can learn only:
   The culture of the outlaw

On the Churchyard Scene in Spring Awakening

1.
Don't shout at the dead
Gravestones have no echo
The dead don't move the folds of their garment
For them Giotto's mouth pursed to paint is a skull's eye
The philosopher's frown frivolous
And the marble monument to their life
A falling leaf

2.
The child sent to play
In the graveyard is killed
By a falling leaf

3.
And do not send your daughters to school with Lot
To hear Judas on death
Learn mathematics from a skeleton telling beads
Where starvation licks the gravel
And love?
Sex! – says the skeleton – try me!

The Headless Boy

When I shot myself
The problem became clearer
But I'd lost the will
To solve it

The problem is always
Their view of you
Which then out of duty
You take
As your view of yourself

But behind their mask
I could be anyone
I have the freedom of Atlas
Who could drop the world on his foot
Or hurl it at their heads

Atlas

Is bent
Under the weight of the world
In the pose
Of the thinker

Or is he doubled up
In laughter?

Bingo

Bingo

Scenes of Death and Money

Blood runs in the athlete's veins
It is also the food of vampires
So is money

And though men don't live by bread alone
Everything else costs money
Money connects all men's activities
And in this way takes-over relationships
So everything becomes a price tag:
The tree bird gun man

A man holds money
As a man under water holds breath
Money is not our element but we live in it
Even our culture is called Capital
We're distorted – fish out of water:
Romantic social political familial artistic industrial cripples

When money controls men
Law becomes crime
And morality a form of violence
Barked by gaolers
And men sow the monstrous growths that grow fat on
    starvation:
Nightmares bombs creeds phantoms weeds hysteria

Caesar wished Rome had one throat
So he could hack it – one blow!
Money is our throat

It is true that men have been saved by love
But they were pushed in the water by hate
Or the boat was jerry built for profit
Or the captain was drunk because he was poor – or rich:
Love is strong only where there is reason

Is it too hard for men to find another system
Not drop the final bombs
Or become the ants of technology?
How do we make freedom?

There is only one way:
    When no man uses another for profit
    He will not need force – he will make no enemies
    He can be guided by sense – not fear or advantage
    He can call all men brothers – for then love will not be
        made sentimental by fraud
    But passionate by reason

So we must face the problems of transition
But those who are afraid of the cure
Die of the disease

Shakespeare and the Beggar

Clothes and hair both rags
Only dirt under the eyes
For tragedy has no passion
To spend on tears

Hands cupped into a bowl
Of wasted flesh to hold
Metal coins

This girl who begs
Her father built my house
Her brother husbanded my fields
Her lover raised my cattle

I own their work
That is: I buy and sell
Their days
Their growing old
Their tragedies and songs
The resilience they learn in snow
Their private whisperings in bed
Their loneliness in the windswept church
Their dignity in death
Their ludicrousness before the judge's soldiers
All sold!
All measured in wages!
For money serves no other interest but its own
Just as necessity drives out other laws

I drop a coin into her hand
And put one by for the hangman
Whose work is also necessity
The last interest due on wealth

It is the custom that you lay
A coin under a dead man's tongue
To pay Charon the ferryman of hell
To ferry him across the river
That springs and dies
At the same source

When I am in his boat
He'll work the coin
Out of my mouth with his fat thumb
Hold it against the moon
Sniff it
Crack it between his teeth
And say: not yours

Then toss me in the Styx
The cloaca of hell

Shakespeare's Last Poem

Last night I dreamed
Of the dry laugh of death
It did not wake me

Look between your teeth
It said
There you'll find crunched
A little black boy

I poked with my finger
My teeth were a cage
Shutting part of me in
And the rest of me out

I jabbed
My teeth snapped
At my own flesh
The little black boy
Fell down my throat

When morning woke me
The sky lit my house
And the wind swept it clean
As it always has

Then I wrote
  You alabaster gods whose eyes don't weep
  But keep their tears for brightness!
  You gods who write laws in the clouds
  Have armies to shield your smiles
  Prisons to guard your temples
  And holy bells that ring
  Like coins being counted

  Those who run after the Unmoving One
  Live in his shadow
  No, to get water
  You dig earth
  Truth can't lie in the well
  Till you've dug it

  Why walk on the water?
  It is easy to swim
  Only the worker rests
  Only the fed are literate
  Only the runner knows where he has been
  Only the fire-eater understands
  Only the sword-swallower is serene
  For history is always hungry

Shakespeare and the Mulberry Tree

The tree needed silence and water
To grow

I made a garden for it
Where only birds sang
And for the tree
That was the sound of water and sun

It grew

One day a man sat under my tree
And murmured gold

Adam and Eve were young
When they lost their garden
I am old
I have opened a gate
That leads to a churchyard

I did not hear the tree's sermon:

Your fingers are like roots
Or
Claws to snatch my mulberries

Eat!

But only roots feed

Other
Eating is excreting

Three poems on Shakespeare

I.
There are no last collections of poems
No personal jottings or summing up
Of nature and politics

The road peters out before the horizon
A worn path to a mirror
That receded

No rustled paper or held breath
Only last walks by the river
And questions

If the poet does not know himself
How can men know each other?
Even love will not last
Unless it is nurtured in the mind
Not left to grow wild in the heart
And there is courtesy in the cities

2.
Uneaten apples rot
Things not consumed are wasted
Things taken pass into knowledge

This world of holes and doors
With its ancient cargo of bones
This world of wind and rain and corners
Where everything changes
Like water in a mill
White and without reflection

At least a coffin takes more wood than a cradle

3.
I have been poisoned by words
That grew in my mouth

I sit under the mulberry tree
The worm sleeps in the sun on my cheek

It knows the geography of my face
The vents and holes under the paper skin

I could regret this or that
Foolish to use my handkerchief
As a shroud for tears

Let those who mourn me cry
(The old woman who ties my chin
Won't cry)

A further Poem on Shakespeare

He is not an academic
His written words
Are the echoes of speech
His learning is prefaced
By experience
He does not come from school
He goes to it

The Fool

The Fool

Culture

All men must answer in their lives
Those questions whose answers are enormous
Because when one man decides how he lives
   He changes all men's lives

There are no small questions for small men
All men are Hamlet on an empty street
Or a windy quay
All men are Lear in the market
   When the tradesmen have gone

No man eats sleeps or loves for himself alone
Harvest and dreams and teaching the young
Don't take place in a small room
   But in the spaces of other men's lives

How we eat decides justice
Our homes measure the perversion of science
Our love controls the meaning of words
And art is whatever looks closely
   In the human face

If there were only irrational ways
To make the world rational
Art would still be reason
   And so our race not left to rot in the madhouse

Reason is the mark of kin
Poetry destroys illusions – it doesn't create them
And hope is a passion that will not let men
    Rest in asylum's peace

On Entering Paradise

If tomorrow the gates of paradise flew open
When you touched them
It would still have cost much blood
    To open them

Look behind you down the long sluice
Of blood and debris of wars past time
And remember this when a voice calls
    How shall we open the gates of paradise?

Blood of itself is not enough
Even in the veins to keep men alive
And spilt it will not make history
    That is the work of reason

But whenever the tongue of reason is cut out
Then violence rises like a madwoman over her toys
Reason is not reborn from her own ashes
Prometheus has been saved a thousand times
    By the vulture that tears his liver

Remember this when you stand at the gates of paradise
And a voice calls from the sluice

Hanged at Ely

No work
Empty bellies
Wet houses
For charity the cold face of the fen

Duties: step out of the carriage way
Pray on sunday
Wait for a war to be paid to kill yourself

What happens?
Resist not evil?
Even the rat that eats a child's face?
We strike the rat away

For that they hang us
Like meat on a butcher's hook
While the judge chews his toothpick
And soldiers harvest with a footpad's knife
For such men reason is a sense of shame!

When the untaught go quietly at the teacher's heels
To the graves
Love does not spring up in the rank shadow of the gallows
To cast out evil

Reason is armed when men cast out reason
For if driven from her home in the human face
She takes up refuge in the human fist

So say the five illiterates hanged at Ely

Clare's Wife

Small and bent lower
Round shoulders in black
Hands bony and clean
As poorman's knife and fork
Her face blank as a scraped plate
Helped by her neighbours since she is stricken
Sometimes she repays in jam
    From the fruit of the medlar tree

She goes to church to be counted
And never to the pub
And all her talk is clichés
A laugh to the carriage trade
A scandal to the schoolmaster
   Absurd in the theatre

Her words are worn steps outside
Stone offices
For her to be articulate would be
Impertinence to a master so skilled in mastery
He uses words to prove language has no meaning
   So the parson brays and the judge gnaws his lip

As she shuts the gates on the asylum
She doesn't speak of incarceration
Her thoughts are muffled by careful footsteps on the gravel
If asked she would say
I make do with what I have and go without what I haven't
   And no man can move her

Mary

A dark woman heavy as earth
Or light as shadows blown in wind

Who?

The woman you bought a ticket for on a bus
Or met once at the foot of a bridge
While the water made a hollow sound in its channel
Like a man under an operation

Not seen for twenty years
You are still taut from touching her

Who?

She is the woman you slept with last night
Who eats at your table
The mother in your house
Who welcomes guests at your door

But you and she are deformed
They tell you: this vacuum is cast for you
So fill it – as if the coffin were the human mould

No, all nature abhors what fills their spaces
The law that watches your bed
The butcher who waits at your table
The pedant waylaying your child at the school door

They took your wife
Now they will take your woman
You are a poet and should have known
You must imagine the real and not the illusion

She will age with your wife's silence
And your dreams bear in shrivelled wombs
The imbecile children who play in senile men

Your woman spent her life under your roof
You never met – not once
In the living room or kitchen
Clare, you created illusions
And they destroy poets

Clare: Autobiography of a Dead Man

Who am I?

I am the play of light
That looks in shadows
Some are as black as crimes
In others I see
    The innocent in their cells

I am the comet
That runs over the night
As a madman
Having the shape of fire
   That breaks and creates

I am the light that goes
Through the machine
Till each steel face
And knot of iron
   Shines as the human face

I know Darkness
When black hands cup the flame
And the night wind howls
   To empty the world

I sat in the asylum chewing bread
I sang: The Sun is a Loaf
Outside it got greyer and people hungrier
If you are still alive and eat
   Remember:

The starving decide the taste of your bread
Prisoners name those to be free
And the poor say who shall have power

So I learned in my cell
And my dark friend in his
   That one day our bread might taste of reason

Clare's Little Songs

I.
The moment when a gate clicks in the night
The clouds huge as mountains
Silent as an empty nursery

A shadow seeking the light
Scuttles along the skirting

The tongue curves like a fish hook
To drag language up from the belly

2.
The hangman leads the dance to the scaffold
One day he will hang himself

The problem of fragments arises
Only when the pot is broken

3.
The man at the door
Saw through the crack
The naked women
Put on clothes
For the wedding

The spring trees
Were wire in the sunlight

4.
When the fool lies on the ground
At the end of autumn

Memory is the dead leaves
That fall from his body

Then the winter serpent steals over the river
His mouth as wide as the ice

5.
In god's room there is a corner
Where his infant toys are thrown
At time thunder rattles from his tin drum
Men are massacred like lead soldiers
He must win victory
Before it is bedtime

6.
Tell someone often enough what they know
And they will forget it

I saw a thrush
Hanged by a living worm

7.
The soldier worried for victory
Goes to the soothsayer
She watches his eyes
While she tells what's written on his head

But he has never looked at himself
Too afraid of the dark!

8.
A singer noticed the notes
Tasted of charcoal

The gypsy who worked the lights
Said: retire

But she sang and sang and learned to sing
With her mouth full of charcoal

9.
The flying knife is a metal bird
Beak — bone handle
It cuts but tastes nothing
Like the mouth of a wound

10.
So many grey teeth and gaps
In the mouth of the mountain

How tired it stands
By the lake

Will it ever fall roaring and hissing
Into the water?

Often!

11.
A squirrel stealing nuts
Sees the giant red sun
Staring through the trees

And pelts it with nuts

12.
Skeletons arguing over
The dice
Came to blows
But couldn't kill themselves

13.
I put my hand in my pocket
And took out a ship

I shook off the water
And set it on the pavement

Inside the hold
Lay a little grey wind

As I walked off
It blew itself home

14.
I heard a strange tune of strings
I searched and found
A fly in a web
Singing to its own destruction

15.
I heard a mole crying beside a pit
I asked it why?
Because you come! Because you come!
The small piece of black earth
Teeth hands and eyes lying in the mud
Useless now

16.
The fields that lie in the morning sun
Hold the mist as a fainting girl
Holds a handkerchief to her eyes

17.
The sun rises over wet grass
In its young splendour

At noon the withered fields
Look like dead cats

The sun falls old
And babbles of itself

But the stream babbled
When it was young

18.
The fool looks for a short cut
To lead people astray
On the march to the madhouse

19.
Morning
The empty cups by the sink
Dead fish

20.
A bird built its nest in the dungeon
From hair of the prisoner's beard

21.
The formal bow to the void
Hands washed before execution
The hangman's pressed trousers

They always carry their dirt
In clean paper

23.
On the welsh hill cleared for pasture
No shade at the low stone wall
Bred for cheap wool thick over the head
Back and sides, in folds on the neck
Piled like carpet
Standing in silent groups
Shaking in shimmering heat
No other motion
Eyes like burned river beds
Silent the heads turn slowly as I pass
Dry mouths open to pant still
As creatures wanting to hide from light

24.
The rabbit's head turns sharply
This way and that

A human skull with fool's ears

25.
The traitor loves the spring
The idler loves summer
The defrauder loves autumn
The hangman loves winter:
    Trees and footprints in snow on the steps

26.
I asked a man drowning puppies at Potters Bar
The London road
He pointed
Then lifted his head to see me

27.
Millions of grass
Bowing before one wind

28.
Waffle waffle little poet
You are mad and don't you know it!

The verse you write could well be worse
You'll still be scribbling in the hearse!

They lock you in this little room
Don't learn the patience of the tomb

29.
Of cities and the roads between them
Of faces that take blows like fists
Of men so small they orate from the top of a mousetrap
Of a world turning as if in a garotte
Of armies sleeping in fields
Of rats that play on the blades of sickles
Of the executioner's towel
    You can make a life
    And no one will ask

We Come to the River

We Come to the River

Soldiers' Song

In the green green grass we lay
As on a lovers' bed
I'll love you Maggie May
While the grass is green I said
O Maggie you were sweet to me
But the grass is wither-ed

O Maggie Maggie May
They have taken you away
For to stay on Van Dieman's cruel shore

Ladies' Anthem

Hail master of war
Hail bringer of peace

Clouds sweep over the battlefield
Over the sacrifice
It is an altar for the fatherland

God has granted the prayer
Uttered by the gun
He gives peace to the fatherland

Children will bless the warrior's old age
He has guarded their laughter
With the sword

Hail protector
Hail giver of freedom and laughter

Officers' Old School Song

When our schooldays are over
We will meet
And live the dreams
We are dreaming now

In the ocean
Who hears the spring?
In the deep
Who hears the waterfall?

Nursery Rhyme

Five sticks and an apple
One head, two arms, two legs
Stick them in: a man!
Throw him, catch him, play
When you're hungry: eat him

First Mad Song

The boat goes over the water
Birds fly from the broken sea
The iron chain drops to the deep
Like a silent killer

Here in the light tears dry on my face
I feel the wind in my mouth
But my child's hands are small
I cannot turn keys or lift burdens
Yet I must pull the heavy oars
So that the boat goes fast through the water

Second Mad Song

Grass grows on the river bank
Rain pours over the white roots
Into the water

Watch the river wander
Over fields
Hiding under bridges

See the trees stretch over the river
No hand comes from the water
To put fruit on the branches

Ministers' Song

Casualties mount and profits rise
But the best of all possible worlds has a flaw
Dead soldiers can't use guns!
What can we do? Careful!
God grant us perfection:
The hunger of the lion and the patience of the spider

Song of the Emperor's Ladies

The beautiful little white clouds
Are baskets of silver fish
The bright sun
Has an iron hook in his mouth

Every night the pale moon rises
A ghost
Weeping and wandering over the polar snow
Hiding from the sun

Song of the Old Woman

Shall I tell you who is weak?
The weak buy men for riches
And sell them for famine
They paint flowers on the desert and call it a garden
They smile like the torturer and bow like the judge
They lead armies to hell so that they shall have a
    kingdom to rule in

Shall I tell you who is strong?
Child, you are strong
You have nothing and your hands are small
But the world spins like clay on a potter's wheel
And you will shape it with these hands

Children's Song

The soldiers shot us
Bang bang you're dead
Why does the wind whistle
In the hole in our head?

Song of the Victims

Child from the river
The water has rocked you
The reeds kept the wind from your head
The wind has sung to you

Child you have slept so still by the river
The earth was a pillow under your head
The reeds have kept the cold wind from you
And men stood watch over your bed

Child do not whimper in your sleep
The dark ice melts in the sun
The rain runs into the river
Spring has begun

A white horse is nibbling the wet grass!
See the silk cradle on its back!
It waits at the path!

The soldiers marched by in the night
Pink flesh in the steel shell
They are lying on the shore
The last order faded away far out to sea
Only birds flying to land heard it

The echo of guns dies on the hills
Tatters of uniform tumble away in the wind
The chains of prisoners are turned into chains for
        anchors
Clowns dance where men stood like sticks
Where the earth was trod to dry circles they heap
        flowers

We stand at the river
If there is a bridge we will walk
If there is no bridge we will wade
If the water is deep we will swim
If it is too fast we will build boats
We will stand on the other side
We have learned to march so well that we cannot
    drown

On Music

Music cannot ask questions
It can startle
That is as good as a question

Music cannot give answers
It can persuade
That is as good as the truth
Music is very dangerous

(We are afraid to believe anything
    Scepticism is polite
        Conviction leads to argument
            Truth loses something if told)

At Auschwitz they hanged men to waltzes
In Chile they broke a musician's hands
With the same irony the church
Once took away heretics' tongues

So there must be a new music
A music you can't hang men to
A music that stops you breaking musicians' hands

On Musicians

Is the patron saint of music Nero?
When the city burns
Should musicians stand
On the roof of the opera house
Bowing and scraping?

Or should they run through the city
Using their instruments as sirens
And singing Fire!

If they find the arsonists
With brands in their hands
Should they call the soldiers
And shout Fire!

You can be sure the arsonists
Have turned off the public conduit
It will be useless
To shout Water!

On the Past

I said to the stone giant
Who sat on the stone bench
Go, you are blocking the street
   His stone hands trembled

I said to him Go
You look in the windows of houses
And frighten children
   Tears fell down his cheeks

He said I'm too heavy to move
I said to him Die
You shut out the sun
Nothing grows
The air is poisoned by slime
That runs from your shadow

He said Inside is my heart

I said Men are born
With two feet in the grave
When they're old
They should have only one foot in it

I had looked at his boots and seen
They were two graves
That's why I killed him

On Our Modern World

It is a matter of interest to see
How long it is before new inventions
Are put to old uses

Electricity is sent through electrodes
Clipped to the body
Men dangled from helicopters on a rope
By college graduates
Medical syringes used in murder
Men dragged at the back of a car
As Achilles dragged Hector round Troy
But Hector was dead
Power drills have efficiently incapacitated
Blow lamps have stripped skin not paint
Flood lamps illumined
What men should shudder to see by day

I speak only of tools of peace
Not weapons of war

   This has nothing to do with you, surely

But your mind is full of modern knowledge
How is it used
In our modern world?

On Enemies

(FOR CHRIS SEARLE)

He's entitled to his opinion
You fight to the death for his right to hold it

If his opinion is that your friend
Must be rubbed out under the heel
Will you fight for his right
To rub out your friend under the heel
Although your friend will be forced
To fight his friend and his enemy?

Perhaps on the last page
The plot of history is solved
And it's shown how true friendship lay
In killing your friend for your enemy's sake

But such paradoxes are beyond me

On the River

When the river winds over the plain
It's a mirror you see your face in
When it runs in a narrow gorge
Or falls with the strokes of a hammer
It foams like a madman as white as smoke
And splinters oaks

   You wind your watch every night
      It won't flatter and say
         It is time
            When you come too late

Do not say you know the river
Because you saw it yesterday
Today it may rain in the mountain
Or the spring sun melt the snow
Do not say you have walked on the water
Perhaps it was only sleeping then
Do not say you have calmed the storm
Perhaps the river was tired from the rapids
And needed to sleep again
Do not say you have captured the river
And dammed it and sluiced it
Perhaps its invisible brother the wind
Which watches you from the treetops
As you pass in and out at your door
Will come to its aid

On Art

On Art 1
Art holds a mirror to nature
Where? Where blind men learn to see

They see themselves in nature
Men in their societies

Men who look straight in the mirror
See the self-portrait of the artist in society

Men who run away see the back of their head
The mirror tells the truth even to faceless men

Art is always in crisis: you must work fast
To write in the breath on the window

On Art 2
Shall I paint the dead?
No use, they made their will long ago
You weren't in it

Shall I write odes to a known beauty?
No, she rotted
She has no favours to give

Shall I write marches for the emperor's armies?
No use
Their dirges have been written

Write for a new age
Of a path that leads away from violence
And isn't guarded at every mile post
By a Class Garrison

Write for the working class
Which needs no chains
Which does not forge the world
To give currency to lies

On Art 3
Newton when old walked on the shore
I have studied these grains of sand
But there (he lifted a finger)
Is the ocean of truth I did not travel
What demons or angels lie in that deep
I know not . . .

   A prisoner reaches from his bunk
     His dirty finger scratches the white wall
       A tree and beside it his name
         As big as the tree

Is the price of freedom all you could have done with it?
Does the longing for reason drive men mad?
No, madmen don't invent a new language
They put words in the wrong order

Barbarians fear beauty and burn it
They imprison the clear mind
Art blackmails civilization

Sand is made by the sea
The storm spends itself on the face of the ocean
Below – the calm

   Behind all art is the smile of the Greek shepherd
   With one sheep on his shoulder

On Art 4
The mirror art holds to nature is cracked
The glass-maker and quicksilver-painter can't mend it

Nature must be mended
Then the mirror will be whole

But look closely at the broken mirror
To see where nature is broken

Art that tells you only who you are
Creates the past

It must tell you who you are
So that you see what you must do

On Art 5
Write about an explosion
By the light of the explosion

Don't wait: you will write of the great beam
That fell on the white horse

And forget how dust forced you to gasp
Till your hand shook

Now while you write the dust in your lungs
Slowly begins to kill

If you had written
By the light of the explosion

You would have told us your hand shook
And we would have known the killer dust

On Art 6
The hand that uses a pen must be stronger
Than ten Hannibal elephants

You must help to haul the baggage cart
Through the pass

Then you can sit in the grass at the top
And eat with the rest

No one eats unless the cart is hauled
Through the pass

After your meal write
Art is not magic

On Art 7
Whenever you see an artist
Look at him closely

He should look like a man
Who's come round a corner

He should look like a man
Who expects surprises

Who distrusts maps
But carries a map in his pocket

On Art 8
Stone pharaoh sitting in sand
Staring at the Nile outside his reach

A bishop in lamb's pelts
Pointing at martyrs' blood
With one hand and the other
Writing an order:
A marble man for the top of my tomb

A merchant buying a still life
Peaches apples delph jug viol
Things bought and sold

Rulers shown a picture of their mind
To prove who they are

Now – a new art
Show who the working class are
And their right to be it

On Art 9
The good writer went on the straight route to heaven
St Peter answered his knock and asked: Who?
I: said the writer
And when he got to the palace of god
He found this sign: To Let

So he had to go all the way down again

On Art 10
The bad writer went on the long route to heaven
When he arrived St Peter asked: Who?

The writer was too short of breath to answer

Saint Peter said: Who? so often
All the angels came to the ramparts to see

Never before had someone had such a reception

On Art 11
A man set out to climb the hill
On the edge of his country

When he reached the top he saw
A hill ahead of him
Blue in the distance
Its forests like shadows

He climbed to the top of the hill
And saw the next hill on the horizon
Sun shone on the snow and ice-clouds
Driven by storms

He climbed many hills
Each hill a blindfold
Stretched over the sky
From end to end of the horizon

When he was old he reached the top of a hill
His eyes were too weak to see
The next wall of rock
He sat on a stone and said
I have reached the plateau

Those who came after
Were comforted by his smile
As they passed on the road

On Art 12

Tell us the Way of the Books
The Manifold Path of Enlightenment
The Discipline of the Mean
The Abstract of all Knowledge
Give us the Key
Come down from the mountain
With Stones of Eternal Truth
  So we can ride to market
  Eat at the scrubbed table
  Used for courts martial
  And get on with our lives
  As if nothing had happened

On Art 13
Avoid a grain in the eye
A splinter in the foot
A fishbone in the throat
    Lest you die to the ways of this world
    And have to seek another

On Art 14
Truth doesn't need a guardian
It's given away in the market place
And no one takes it

On Art 15
There is no special language of poetry
A workman's tools are the simplest
That will do the work
Otherwise the tool would waste
The workman's effort
    A poet is as careful

On Art 16
A rational man sees into himself
A cynic sees through himself

When the hangman talks of compromise
He means he will shorten the rope

The only empathy in art
Is love of justice

On Art 17
A rock starts an avalanche
By using its weight
To stay on the mountain

Wishes may be beautiful
But plans have
A touch of ugliness in them

On Art 18 : The Electric Chair

i.
It is scrubbed
New warders sit in it
High laughter

Always two things for force:
To hang – a hard beam and a coiled rope
Here – wood blocks and wire

An order, a response

ii.
The assistant has not painted
The headrest with skulls
The executioner is a craftsman
Not an artist

iii.
This chair kills
It could not create
A midwife could rest her basin on it
But art is not a chance collection
Of happenings
The image changes the pattern

iv.
Paint the scene exactly
Record the evidence with care
The chiselled wood
The shadow on the seat
The hue of the light
As a policeman records
The scene of the crime

The image will hold time still
And show the end in the beginning
Then disaster will be seen
To be caused

v.
Paint the chair with the body in it
Dressed in prison white
The uniform of a ghost
Straps hold him upright
But he has misplaced himself
In the straps
The head is hooded
But the hands show an expression

This is a still-life
With a reason

vi.
In this world cause and effect
Are not crime and punishment
In art cause and effect
Are act and reward
Art shows change in a moment
It is the still life of change

The man who runs fastest
Leaves fewest footprints

vii.
They tied him down in a harness
And made him leap
Even before he came to this place

They break their own bones when they fall
They break the bones of others when they rise
No wonder they broke his bones
They broke him before he came here
Today they broke only his neck

This is their execution shed
What do they call their city?

Stone

Stone

First Chorus

Men are not asked who they are but ordered to be
Cut to the shape of a square world
And the head bound as surely as old China
Bound women's feet

Why this unreason?

The tool-user makes tools for his purpose
They work – no questions!
They break – new ones!

Just make enough money to drown your voice
Turn on enough light to blind you
Block out the windows with light
Run long enough to learn how to sleep on the run
This is the first obligation on all tools:
Don't know your own function

So what weight presses you to the ground?
Why does the young hand shake with the palsy of
   age?

What is the definition of a tool?
A space that exactly fills its own prison

Song of False Optimism

Goliath was bigger than a mountain
David killed him with a stone
Goliath fell down like a landslide
David was light on his feet
He saw the shadow fall over him
And stepped aside just in time

David knelt to thank the lord
Goliath in the kicks of death
Raised his fist – it came down like a shell
David had good hearing
He heard the mighty rushing of wind
And stepped aside just in time

David sang a victory song
Out of the hole in Goliath's head
An evil gas poured over the world
David had a good sense of smell
He smelt the air turning septic
And got out of that just in time

David danced a dance of praise
When Goliath was struck his spear had spun
High in the air – it came down like a bomb
David had a good sense of touch
He felt the tip scratch the top of his skull
And stepped aside just in time

Merlin and Arthur

Merlin was a great wizard
He took eggs from the air
He took a loaf from a beggar's sleeve
He even made a corpse smile
By letting it smell his finger

King Arthur was a jealous king
He took the loaf and eggs
The dead man had been his worst enemy
He'd killed him in battle
So he hanged Merlin for treason

Song of the Seven Deadly Veils

How is society organised?
For the happiness of the people?
Or so that profit can be drawn
At as many points as possible?
What d'you want out of the cow?
Milk or blood?
Then stop sticking your knife in
All over its hide

The Governor begging at the widow's door
The soldier as protector of the poor
The strongman waiting humbly for the weak
The spokesman who gives up his turn to speak
When things like this are seen
The world will be a better place
Than it has been

    Evil creates its own remedy!
    Till then we stagger round and lose our breath
    In that old side show called The Dance of Death!

In the famous dance of the seven deadly veils
Bad turns to good
Homes turn to jails
Can turns to should
A corkscrew is straight
Saints turn to whores
But don't send to ask whose head is on the plate:
   It's yours!

The priest and teacher whisper together
Mankind is a tragic animal
Destined by nature to fight forever
Man against man with tooth and claw
But our pyramids!
Will this brawling pack ever get them built?
Call in the overseer!

The working man who gets some time for thought
The thinker whose conclusions can't be bought
The office seeker who can use a spade
The specialist who cures before he's paid
When things like this are seen
The world will be a better place
Than it has been

Evil creates its own remedy!
Till then we stagger round and lose our breath
In that old side show called The Dance of Death!

In the famous dance of the seven deadly veils
Bad turns to good
Homes turn to jails
Can turns to should
A corkscrew is straight
Saints turn to whores
But don't send to ask whose head is on the plate:
    It's yours!

All men must work or scheme to get money
To buy food and shelter for their families
The Greatest Profit is king of this jungle
That's how vices become virtues
What follows?
When the judge's throat is cut
It's done by his own law!

The scientist who builds his life on truth
The judge who convicts only after proof
The son who never bore his father's curse
The king who doesn't ride behind a hearse
When things like this are seen
The world will be a better place
Than it has been

  Evil creates its own remedy!
  Till then we stagger round and lose our breath
  In that old side show called The Dance of Death!

  In the famous dance of the seven deadly veils
  Bad turns to good
  Homes turn to jails
  Can turns to should
  A corkscrew is straight
  Saints turn to whores
  But don't send to ask whose head is on the plate:
    It's yours!

Bad Dream

The white cliffs that stand by the sea –
Every night the black water stirs itself
And leaves its bed
And seizes the cliffs
And takes them down to a hole
Under the sea
And in the dark like a blind torturer
It tortures them with pain and supplice
And before there is light it sends them back
To the edge of the sea

And they stand and stare at the black water
Stirring listlessly in its sleep
All day

Song of Naivety

When I left home my parents
Gave me seven coins for the journey
They said if the journey is long
And these coins don't reach
Look in your soul
There you will find
All that is needful

To thine own self be true
The rest will follow

Song of Experience

You come smiling to offer service
You bring two good hands to help
Your face is open and guileless

But you find you are too weak to help
The grain you wanted to take to the farmers
Is in a tower – with guards at the door

You haven't even got the things that are yours
To get them you have to fight
The steps of your journey measure out a duel
And the weapons are chosen by your enemy

Grandma Faust

Grandma Faust

Paul's Songs

Spiritual

Lawd I have a hollow chest
How the wind he howl in my hollow chest
He whistle in my hollow chest
Like a beggar man call his dog

Lawd I dress in ter'ble rags
How the wind he love my ter'ble rags
He dress his self up in my ter'ble rags
An dance like he's dancin for the lawd

Lawd I have these bare bare bones
How the wind he play with my bare bare bones
He done rattle my bare bare bones
Like he nailin down the coffin of the world

Lawd I work in the cotton field
This cotton field clothe half the world
This white white sheet is my windin sheet
When the lawd he done fetch me home

Lawd I travel by the water side
I sings like a bird an I hops an glide
The river can't sing but it still roll on
I wonder do it know the direction of the tide

Last Song

Little silver fish for my soul an me
Dancin t'gether in the bright blue sea
A golden apple bouncin on the tree
Pick it an eat it an you will be free

When the river's as wide as it is long
It'll be a sea for ships to sail on
When waves are as high as the sea is broad
They'll flush out the devil an drown the lawd

Now here's the moral of this here show
Wise man said a long time ago
No man step in the same river twice
Why the fish his world just flow away!
Ain no knowed way of making it stay
How's your world folks? You snug in bed?
Once every day your world stand on its head

The Swing

The Swing

On Being an Optimist: a Wall Poem

There's a solution to every problem
The solving of which would make the world better

But to do one thing right
You may need to do
Four things wrong
Don't let the four things
Stop the one thing

And though you lived in a time
When for one right thing
A hundred wrongs have to be done
Seize the chance!
Do the one thing!
Or the things that are wrong
Will be one hundred and one

(An earlier version of this poem was chalked on the auditorium wall of the Almost Free Theatre for the first production of The Swing, *November 1976)*

Tale of the Mississippi

Three hundred years
Boats work the river
Carry cotton an cattle
Traders built wharves on the bank
An houses an factories in the interior
An all sorts of slaves
    Is sold in the markets

That is a good river
Mighty an strong as blood
By night lights on the steamers
Cigar smoke an banjos
There was crimes in the darkness
Bodies drop overboard
Slaves hunted down in the swamp
    But no more than any place else

One day the river stop
People stare down in the water
Bottom's hid by the mud
Ain never look down afore
River start t' rise
A flood lays waste the interior
Cattle an people git drown
Seemed as if the survivors
    Come out of the river itself

Three hundred years mud
Built at the mouth of the river
Then just like it started
T' slowly shake its head
That river scattered its waters
It is a mighty river
    An that day it own the earth

The Walls of Paradise

As too many are born for the keeper of paradise to know
     their faces
He has a list of names and records of lives
The devil gave the keeper the name of a good man
The keeper looked up the name in the list and opened the
     gates to the devil
This led to ten hundred thousand years of war
In the end they managed to bind the devil and throw him
     out
The keeper adopted a new procedure
Anyone who wants to get into paradise stands at the wall
The keeper shouts: Name!
When the honest man answers the keeper opens the gate
The liar is found out: lies have no echo
Only truth echoes on the walls of paradise or anywhere
     else

The State of the World

The judge understands
That the poor rob the rich
How could it possibly be
That the rich rob the poor?
D'you ever find rich men in prison?

The teacher understands
That the taught teach the untaught
How could it possibly be
That the illiterate have lessons to teach?
Can facts contradict themselves?

The general understands
That armies are strong
How could it possibly be
That the weak could win battles?
Do the weak have armies?

The priest understands
Why god's sometimes slow in speaking
How could it possibly be
That he who sees all could make quick decisions?
Could men make a better world?

If the poor and untaught and weak made the world
There would be superstition famine and war

Heraclitus

Heraclitus said no man steps in the same river twice
The cripple's crutch changes at every step
The dog barks always for a new master

You cannot choose your destination
You can choose to start the journey
When you are lost
You may be travelling with those who have found the way

The Spider

Once was a spider sleek an fat
Said I'll build me a web on a corner of the palace
Sure was a number one spider
Worked harder than a rat

Got hisself a web so big it spread out the winder
Took over the whole palace
Then the streets where folks works
Then where they lives
Took the lot – then more

After that it really spread
First one country then the rest
Spider sure was a spider out the ordinary
But the whole thing was gettin to his head

Spider was way down deep in the web
Carryin out necessary maintenance
Holdin it together
Churnin thread

The flies was on the outside
Dying like flies natch
But spider he couldn't git to his dinner nohows
Just shrivelled up
Then he was dead

That web sure was a fine piece of engineerin technology
But folks! – who'd have thought it'd turn out to be
The wrappins of a mummy?

Change

Time has two faces: never and always
So we face only one direction

History has two hands: right and wrong
How else could it carry such heavy burdens?

Justice has one law: slaves outnumber masters!
Can an elephant be a parasite on a flea?

The truth is strong because it changes
Lies are eternal: that's how they're found out

Will slaves wait in patience while masters dress up like
    gods?
Who taught the dog to roll on its back to get rid of fleas?

Whoever looks at the clock becomes angry
It is painful to ask the time – or tell it

Do men believe lies when the clocks are hidden?
Time is still told

Imagine

Imagine a country where most things
Belong to one people and others get little

Imagine that lies and violence are used
So people don't ask for their share

It's hard to imagine? But imagine it!
Are you safe? Or what happens?

Imagine gangsters conspiring to carve up a city
Each gets one share

Justice requires the subtle distinctions
Made by courteous low-speaking men

Do you imagine you can discover the way
To deal out injustice justly?

Are you safe? Gangsters shoot one another
That is what happens

The Sins of the Fathers

An unjust act doesn't offend god's laws
It offends its victim
That's why there's justice in this world
The prophet who sees justice
As a ray shining here from the hereafter
Takes the moon's image on water
For a candle under the sea

Time is impatient!
Let the beggar bite the hand that feeds him
Let the poor break the fist that beats them
Otherwise they are also beaters and starvers
Punishing their sins in their children
For generations.

Running an Unjust City

An unjust city is chaos!
Violence rumour envy and crime!

The ruler of an unjust city
Needs great efficiency and persistence
Unsleeping observation and swiftness in action

But these are the talents of rational men
The unjust city is weak
It has only fools to protect it

To the Sons of Unjust Fathers

You have been promised the old possessions
They have been secured by lawyers
Guards will be paid to hand them over

An accumulation of great riches!
Vigour and ease
An athlete's body
A firm hand
And smiles
Yours! And even the poor
Are not wholly bitter
About the past

But you will get nothing
Unjust men destroy by method
Whatever has beauty or goes well
And unjust fathers cut down their sons
From habit

The Swing

The scales of justice are a seesaw
No man holds the balance

You sold the innocent yesterday
Today the guilty sing and kick down your door

The old seamstress died in your workshop of sweated labour
Her daughter will kill your son with a thread picked up on
    the shop floor

The thief knocks at night
Who opens the door of your mansion? You!

The scales of justice are a seesaw

When you are brought down to plead to be serious
The goddess of justice will laugh

No man holds the balance

You may bribe all the judges
You can't blackmail one executioner

Justice carries a sword
And a bucket of water

No man holds the balance

You rise on the seesaw
The other end falls like a hammer

To a Racist

1.
A wizard believes his own magic
His proof? Others believe it

Make the lie big enough and it will move mountains
But who puts their house in order
By starting an earthquake?

Magicians deceive the eye
Wizards deceive the mind

2.
The oldest trick in the world!
Tap a man on one shoulder
And rob his other pocket

   How many leaders point at the future with one hand
   While the other gropes for the past!

The second oldest trick in the world!
Go to a man with arms flung open
Smile and embrace him
And put a knife in his back

How often the man who destroys you
Greets you as friend!

3.
You are strong but a few mice at night
Gnaw holes in your cupboard
And devour your food
    Drive them out!

Then you'll be given all you are promised
    Drive them out!

So the great hunt starts: ten mice are slain
A little grey heap at the door
    Next day two

The food is still taken!
Who hides the mice?
Someone in the family?
Your son? Arrest!
Where is the hideout?
Tear up the skirting!
The floorboards!
Pull down the roof!

You sit in the ruins
Filthy and silent
You don't move when the rats come
Not even when they scuttle
Over your feet

4.
A game has rules
Cheating also has rules
The cheat learns a new set of rules

When you use these rules
You play the game called lying

You will find the prizegiver
Also lies

5.
Politics is the art of the possible
Are they playing a game
Making impossible horror possible
Making the unnatural common in the light of day?

Would it cost more pain and struggle
To work for the vision of peace
And build the impossible on earth?

6.
They say each night a bird flies over the city
Scattering coins
The streets are littered with gold

But the strangers who see in the dark
Pick up the coins while you sleep
In the morning the streets are bare
And your children cry

Drive them out! – Look! a body
How natural – an unemployed father
Beats up a stranger!
(Even by day they prowl the streets:
A coin might be left)

The day you drive out the strangers
The streets won't be littered with gold
They'll be splashed with blood
And your children will still cry

Must the voice of the man in the street
Always come from the gutter?

7.
I cannot blame you for ignorance
To a corkscrew straight lines are bent

You have imbibed from the zealot
And drunks reel

Even in the grey morning you want the bottle
Not argument

Someone who broke the bottle over your head
Would do you a service

I defend this seeming unreason
Reason does not incite madmen to madness

8.
I take you to the edge of your little grave

I show you: it is a mass grave

There's your dead wife nursing your dead child
There are the broken hands of your parents
The unrecognizable faces of friends

Your eyes are glazed with not seeing

Can you step out of the way
When I show you the grave at your feet?

This Century

I.
In this century a conveyor belt
Was built for death

We wasted everything
But nothing more than human lives

That's how we'll be remembered: heaps of bodies
On sidings and outside gates

But our century was also the time when slaves
Turned their masters' ploughshares to swords

When people learned to tell facts
In everyday language

When myths painted over the faces of idols
Were seen to run in the rain

So even the century of progress
Made the world better!

This was our fault:
We had the chance
To change the old world to a new world
Yet we waited

2.
The dead were buried by bulldozers

Scientists discovered the way of the locust
They stripped trees bare

We suffered the diseases of affluence
Others were left to starve

Cancer came out of nowhere –
They say all plagues do

In our time history's pages
Were turned by firestorms

Yet we went on our daily business
Read children to sleep in the shelters

We ate and learned how to work
We washed our linen

How strong we must have been!
Or – the dead say —— how lucky

3.
A roman emperor went to the games
He said he wanted to see
The worst his age had to offer

We saw the worst on our street corners
In the arena we learned a simple lesson
    When children starve in peacetime
    That should be called war

4.
In the past Light Age followed Dark Age
In seemly progression

We live in an age of great darkness
And great light

We use knowledge to give fools reason for folly
As much as to make men wise

What a giantess truth is when her shadow
Throws so much darkness
And her stirrings cause such confusion!

From an Unfinished Ballet

From an Unfinished Ballet

Pity

There is enough pity to go round
The problem is whom to pity
It is no solution to pity everyone
Some people are the reason why others are pitied

If pity is the motive for action
It is unjust to pity everyone
Such pity is callous

The rain falls on the just and the unjust
But the roofs of the unjust keep out water
War ends for the general and the soldier
But who retires in peace?
The tide turns for the fed and unfed
But who eats the silver fish?

It is unjust to pity the poor
It is just to change their condition
It is just to pity the rich
Their condition is going to be changed

The Shepherd

The good shepherd protects the sheep from the wolf
And delivers them up to the butcher

Sheep! take pity on yourselves
Savage the shepherd when he comes
To count his flock with his crook

In the heat of the afternoon
The shepherd sits on the grassy bank
And plays to you on his pipes

He is more wolf-like than the wolf
Look! on his shoulders the hide of a kid

He will carry you on his shoulders
Feet trussed for his brother the butcher

When you are lost
He will go back over the road
Like a man who has dropped
His purse

A Factory Owner to His Son

Call no man happy till he's dead
That's what the Greeks said

Let's hope their optimism
Is justified

Meanwhile make the most of what the other man's
    got
And by the sweat of his brow earn your bread

The owner of the artificial limb factory
Can afford philanthropy in time of war

In the darkest hour the road turns
For better or worse

Take whatever chance the gods offer
When they wake from their nap

Digest the universal law
The arts of peace flourish in war:
  Bread is made by guns!

The Order of Things

The priest with his leaf of statistics
Raises his finger and leans from the pulpit
Like a clown poking out of a coffin
Calling the people damned
While his brother-in-law the butcher
Waits at the West Door
With his friend the merchant in slaves
Who sells second hand goods
  These are not the order of things

That the poor steal
That the weak strike their masters
That they do as they are done by
These are the order of things
For justice is a mirror that reverses the order of
    things
  So that the truth is shown

A Crippled Soldier on a Canal Path

The canal runs smoothly in the narrow cut
Between factory backs and warehouses
On the tow path worn by horses
A crippled soldier practises his wooden leg
Where no boys jeer when he stumbles
And no women in fur collars stare

Closing a Health Centre during an Inflation

The just community helps all in need
Belonging to such a community
  Makes everyone whole

But there is no peace in the economic war
The booty can't cover the cost of getting it
In the present economic crisis
  All must sacrifice for all

Victory is won by arming men at the front
Not tending wounded in the rear
  War is not a time for wholeness

In the present economic crisis
  The Centre must close

The committee wanted to keep it open
But we must think of the community
So we said Close!: we decided against ourselves
Your pleading won't make us weep
  We have already wept

No one will be thrown on the streets
The cruel times are past
Cure the patients you have
But let no more in
  The Centre will run down

Reopening a Health Centre

When the administrators wanted to shut the Health
    Centre
Many workers struck to keep it open
The administrators met to discuss the situation
And changed their tactics in the following way

> For ten years Troy withstood the Greeks
> The Greeks waited before the strong gates
> An army of rats entering through the sewer
> Could have nibbled Troy to dust in a year
> We see our error: we said close the Centre
> The sick workers are too weak to resist
> But the workers outside know
> There are accidents everyday in the factories
> So the strong have come to the aid of the weak
> > Shall we sit in front of this human wall
> > Like the Greeks at Troy?

Let us keep the Centre open
To show we are moderate and humane
Instead we will close ten schools
(If pupils resist we'll say they're hooligans)
Wards in old people's homes must take more
    beds
(The senile dont need much space)
Welfare services can be trimmed
(Who sees into the back rooms of houses?)
There are so many ways we can get the money
> The class that rules isn't the class that makes
>   no errors
> But the class that knows the errors it makes

It seems the workers should meet again
And reconsider their tactics

A Song of Tactics

The end for which you fought for years
For which your comrades gave their lives
Is about to fall into your hands
And then might come the moment to let it go
The day you arrive to enter the house you built
Might be the day to burn it or let your enemy use it
Hannibal spent eighteen years marching on Rome
One evening he stood within sight of its walls
He watched from a hill for an hour – then turned back
Rome was taken by another route
At another time

Then you begin to learn that hope which moves
        mountains
(Yes – everyday!) is not for hire at low rates of pay
    The potter who makes the beautiful white vase
    Labours with hands in clay

Who can pass the child left to drown by the river?
But who feeds the tenth child? Or shelters the
        hundredth?
Who owns the river? Whose fields
Does its water make fertile?
Today the river is calm and smiling
Why do the people who live on its banks
Shiver as though they were trapped by a flood?
While you are asking the landlord these questions
For the sake of the child – the child might drown
But ask and be answered

Then you begin to learn that hope which moves
        mountains
(Yes – everyday!) is not for hire at low rates of pay
    The potter who makes the beautiful white vase
    Labours with hands in clay

Chorus to Peace

War is a frightened child
It runs over the fields
Shouting 'Peace!'

Listen – it runs from dead to dead
Crying 'Peace!'

O pity the infant War lost in the fields
Who will not dry its tears?

The world is small
We have all seen the faces of everyone in it

Will no one lead the infant War
To its mother Peace?

*

Lion cannot sleep with lamb
But brother need not rend brother
The child must learn the wisdom of men
And age and die
But no man need sweat in another's hire
Or learn the lore of the beast with his fodder
A starving man would sell the world for a penny
The rich ask more when they sell a man
Justice is simple
It cannot be bought or sold
And where there is justice
No man can be bought or hired or sold

*

In those days fathers will take their sons to the hills
Where battles were fought
And bones lie under
The silver birches
That shake in the wind
And their sons will not be sent to kill families
On a day they dont even record in a diary
And children will play on the hill
And pity will smile

The Bundle

These nine poems come from a longer series. All the poems in this series are published with the play.

E.B.

The Bundle

Who Can Choose?

Each man walks out his life in his small circle
Lifted from his cradle by elders
Borne to his grave by sons
And in that small circle
Works and laughs
Argues for or against reason
Loves and mourns
And is made weaker or stronger by neighbours

He is born in his spring and dies in his winter
But his seasons are ruled by other men's lives
Who can choose?

Great storms rock his chair
Or he opens his door to the fury
Avalanches gently push him one step
Or he leaps over cracks as they open in mountains
Seas wash his hands or he swims through them
Armies whisper into his ear
Or he asks who leads them and why they fight
He sleeps in his quiet world
Or goes out to the cry in the street
He waits till the storm batters his house
And crowds stand at his door
Or he asks: what is justice?

He can choose

Crimes

The unjust temper injustice with pity
The merciless give mercy
Just as tradesmen to make a profit
Mark some goods down

Those who teach ignorance
Endow libraries
And found great colleges
To teach it in

Barbarians patronize art
Would you expect the rich
To keep ugly whores?

Many shout peace!
Before their armies banners flutter
As if an invisible hand
Was struggling to rip them off
And throw them away

Perhaps this is their greatest crime –
Not the centuries of exploitation and violence
But their occasional use of virtue?

First World War Poets

You went to the front like sheep
And bleated at the pity of it
In academies that smell of abattoirs
Your poems are still studied

You turned the earth to mud
Yet complain you drowned in it
Your generals were dug in at the rear
Degenerates drunk on brandy and prayer
You *saw* the front – and only bleated
The pity!

You survived
Did you burn your generals' houses?
Loot the new millionaires?
No, you found new excuses
You'd lost an arm or your legs
You sat by the empty fire
And hummed music hall songs

Why did your generals send you away to die?
They saw a Great War coming
Between masters and workers
In their own land
So they herded you over the cliffs to be rid of you
How they hated you while you lived!
How they wept over you once you were dead!

What did you fight for?
A new world?
No – an old world already in ruins!
Your children?
Millions of children died
Because you fought for your enemies
And not against them!

We will not forget!
We will not forgive!

Poem

They run the clinic in which you're born
Christen you in their church
Teach you the rules of their school
Examine your minds
Mark them
Donate your playing field
Teach you the rules of their games
Employ you and pay you
Pay you when there's no work
Print your money
Marry you in their church or their registry office
Christen your children
Censor your television
Let you listen to their radio
Share their newspapers with you
Sweep your street
Train your police
Give you medals
Encourage you with bonuses
Punish you when you're a nuisance
Put you in hospital when you're sick
Take you into care when you're old
Burn you in their crematorium
And scatter your ash on their grass

No wonder some of you fight for them
When the rest start to ask
What the hell they're doing!

De Qué Sirve una Taza?

You knock out the teeth
Twist the neck till the skin is taut
Like wrinkles on ice
Scorch the hair as you do on a pig
Tie the hands
And break them with a hammer
Dress the body in rags
As if it were a wound
Empty the skull
And stuff it with sheets
Torn from your book
Shoot out the eyes
So the face looks like cracked glass
And now you offer a cup

What use is a cup?

The Water Seller and the Soldier

On the street the water seller
Meets a soldier and his prisoner
The prisoner asks for water
But has no money to buy it

Though the soldier forbids the water seller
To give the prisoner water
The water seller could bribe the soldier
But he is poor and must sell his water

And though the soldier
Would arrest the water seller
If he smiled to comfort the prisoner
As it is forbidden to fraternize with prisoners
(Unless the water seller had bribed the soldier
To permit him to smile at the prisoner –
An event so unlikely it can be discounted
Even by poets)
It so happens that the water seller
Does not choose to smile at the prisoner
(Or anyone else for that matter)
Because lately many water sellers' water
Was stolen on this very street

Thus the soldier defends the water seller
So that his trade may prosper
And his life be happy and good
But the water seller can't do this good deed
Nor even smile
(Had he chosen to smile)
Because the soldier defends him

So the water seller and the soldier
Smile at each other

Is this the behaviour of rational beings?

Culture

What is culture?
The best? – Too vague!

Who owns the tool?
The man with money
Who uses the tool?

The tool user
What does the tool do?
Change the relationship
Between men and the world
Who owns the tool user?
The man with money
What does the tool do?
Change society
What is society?
The relationship between
Owner and user

What is culture?
Taking power from the owner
To give to the user
That is culture
The highest the human mind
Can aspire to!
The passing of power
From owner to user
Creates virtue and art
Nothing else raises
Men over the beast
Whatever hinders this passing of power
Is against culture
Culture is this change

What is Wanted

I wanted to smile
But I saw how the evil smiled
I wanted to share
But I learned that long after I'd given
All I had
The poor would be poor
I did not want anger
I'd heard of the saint who found freedom in prison
But this only comforts gaolers
Above all I wanted peace
For I knew war

But what I wanted is not yet to be had
Now I want something else:
That one day it will be

For that I would give up
All I had wanted

Essay on the Sellers of Water

1.
Water sellers sell water to the poor
The groans of the poor are pitiful
Why don't the water sellers give water
At least to the poorest?

In the merchant world everything is priced
A green paper fluttering in the storm
Is scrap or a banknote –
Which is decided by the world of the merchant
Though both flutter like a leaf in the storm

Men too flutter in the storm
And whether they're scrap or worth money
The world of the merchant decides

2.
Every commodity has a price
The price tags are clear to be seen on the counter
But in the world of the merchant all things are priced
Acts thoughts dreams regrets – all priced
Just as all things on earth cast a shadow

It is a law:
When one thing is priced all things are priced
The water seller prays for drought
To keep up the price of water
And so he prays that the world of the merchant stands
        firm
And therefore that all things shall keep their price

See! the water in the bowl
Creates the water seller
He earns his life by selling water
His life is shaped by the laws of selling
His world lives by the laws of selling
His morals are based on the laws of selling
All his laws are laws of selling!

If the water seller can't give his water
At least he can smile at the poor?
No! – when one thing is priced all things are priced
To give water ruins the price of water
To smile freely destroys the value of virtue
It replaces the law of selling with a new law
But in the world of the merchant
Virtue depends on the price of water
So to smile you must first change the world
The man who smiles does not wish to sell water
The water seller can only simper or grin

3.
The merchant thinks that at evening
He shuts his shutters and goes – leaving the market
No! – the whole of his life is bought and sold
His world is a tree that roots in the market
The topmost leaf and the smallest twig
Grew from its gutter

The merchant is like a boy in an apple tree
When the wind blows his body contorts
His arms stiffen like branches
The apples hang from his hands
The wind blows through him
And he has become part of the tree
He may reach for the highest apple
But the wind still blows or the bough bends
And shapes the boy to the tree

The merchant believes he has hours of peace
And contemplation after the takings are checked
No! – even time flows like water from the municipal conduit
In the market square
Guarded by marble statues of commerce and providence
All all! follows the same law
Even contemplation is sold in the market
Even silence and stillness
Religion virtue culture and love
All buying and selling
Bubbling and seething

4.
And one day the spring water rises
And sweeps the merchants and soldiers out to the ocean
Like rubbish thrown over a mountain

There is also this law:
When one thing is not priced nothing is priced
The water carried to the streets is not changed
But the laws are changed
The powers that force the laws are changed
The men that carry the water are changed

The spring water rises and merchants and soldiers are
    swept away
Like trash thrown behind a mountain
And the value of water is judged
Not by what it earns
But the thirst it quenches
And all things are changed

To the Readers

For two days as I finished
The book of these poems snow fell

How bright the green showed
In the snow

And how silent the footsteps
Of passers-by

As if men had learned at last
To reverence the world